ACKNOWLEDGEMENTS

Thanks to Ron Benrey, author of *The Complete Idiot's Guide to Writing Christian Fiction,* for teaching me the concept of plotting using the 13 plot points, and James Scott Bell for the foundational structure of plotting presented in *Plot & Structure.* Thanks also to Tom Chiarella author of *Writing Dialogue.* Great examples and instruction, Tom. I also recommend readers pick up a copy of *Dialogue* by Gloria Kempton. Finally, thanks to Steven James for his writing insights. His book *Story Trumps Structure: How to Write Unforgettable Fiction by Breaking the Rules* should be on the desk of ever novelist.

DISCLAIMER

This book includes instructional materials, notes, and handouts for workshops I've taught at a number of writers' conferences. The intent of this book is to present the basic elements of novel writing in UNDER 60 MINUTES. In other words, it is a SHORT book. Do not expect lengthy explanations or examples of how to use these techniques. Think of this book as Cliff's Notes© for a novelist.

When your plot sags, dialogue drags, or scenes feel stale, pull out this book and review the basics. Chances are, a quick review will reveal the issue and inspire you to push on.

For 2015 we've added basic plotting tips for writing a cozy mystery and romantic comedy. Again, do not look for examples or lengthy descriptions of how to flesh out characters, etc. I teach this material in 50-minute classes and we move fast. By the way, much of the romantic comedy formula can be adapted to writing basic romance.

If you find this book helpful please post a review on Goodreads, Amazon, and Barnes and Noble. Your comments are appreciated.

TABLE OF CONTENTS

Chapter 1

WHAT IS PLOT?..1

Conflict 2

Story Summary 3

Power of Experience 5

Power of Desire 5

Who Is Your Lead? 5

Conflict = Tension 7

Internal and External Conflict...................... 7

Inner vs. Outer 8

Character Conflict 8

Driven to Disrupt..................................... 8

Problems = Energy 8

Pacing and Pulse 9

Hope vs. Fear 10

Knockout = Success................................. 10

The Great Disturbance.............................. 10

Plot In Action! 11

Example of Plot in Action 16

Chapter 2

DRAMATIC DIALOGUE 19

    Function of Dialogue 20

    Elements of Dialogue 20

    Reflective Dialogue 21

    Misdirected Dialogue 21

    Modulated Dialogue 23

    Breathless Dialogue 24

    Compressing Dialogue 25

    I Have Rhythm 25

    Circle Back 26

    The Silent Treatment 27

    Dramatic Gesture 27

    Unique Gesture 28

    Incidental Gesture 28

    Directed Dialogue 28

    Parent, Adult, Child 29

    Do's and Don't s of Tags 30

    Punctuation 31

    7 Essentials for Dialogue............................ 33

Chapter 3

CREATING COMPELLING CHARACTERS 35

    Building Characters................................... 36

    Goals for Your Lead 36

    Want, Need, Motivation 36

    The Journey of Your Lead........................... 37

    Depth of Your Lead 37

    S t r e t c h Your Lead................................. 37

A NOVEL IDEA

LEARN HOW TO WRITE A NOVEL IN UNDER 60 MINUTES

Eddie Jones

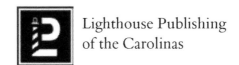

Lighthouse Publishing
of the Carolinas

A NOVEL IDEA: LEARN HOW TO WRITE A NOVEL IN
UNDER 60 MINUTES BY EDDIE JONES
Published by Lighthouse Publishing of the Carolinas
2333 Barton Oaks Dr., Raleigh, NC, 27614

ISBN: 978-1-941103-54-8
Copyright © 2015 by Eddie Jones

Available in print from your local bookstore, online, or from
the publisher at: www.store.lpcbooks.com

For more information on this book and the author visit:
EddieJones.org

Library of Congress Cataloging-in-Publication Data
Jones, Eddie.
Learn How to Write a Novel in Under 60 Minutes / Eddie
Jones 3rd ed.

Printed in the United States of America

PRAISE FOR *A NOVEL IDEA*

This book promises to teach the elements of a novel in under an hour. Clear, concise explanations and lots of white space that invites the reader to pause and absorb the information allows it to do just that.

~Lisa Hess
Author of *Casting the First Stone*

I was curious, and for the money, what could I possibly lose by adding this little book to my stockpile of writing references? This may be the shortest book on crafting fiction that's ever been written, but it didn't advertise itself as more than a tidbit, un soupcon, shall we say, of writing tips. It certainly didn't claim to be exhaustive. In reality, it offered – in those well-laid-out points – a valuable checklist for each of us, no matter how many stories we've written..

~ Normandie Fischer
Author of *Becalmed,* and *Sailing Out of Darkness*

For such an inexpensive book, I found a wealth of helpful information in "A Novel Idea!" Author Eddie Jones has compiled concise guidelines for all the aspects of developing a novel that will keep a reader consumed in your book. Everything from character development to dialogue to developing a memorable scene is covered, with moments of humor to keep a reader laughing. "A Novel Idea" should be used as a checklist for every author to compare their missives before submitting to a publisher.

~ **Elaine Marie Cooper**
Award-winning author of *Fields of the Fatherless* and the
Deer Run Saga

I know this book is presented as the written material for a class taught at writing conferences, but I found the info in here invaluable! Eddie Jones has a gift of breaking down information into manageable, repeatable bites. His insights are spot on and his delivery makes the book a great read.

~ **Edie Melson**
Author of *Connections* and
Fighting Fear: Winning the War at Home When Your Soldier Leaves for Battle

Consequences for Your Lead 38

Creative Trust..38

Pulling for the Hero 40

Care Comes First 40

How to Make the Reader Care 41

Making a Character 41

Predisposition 41

At Rest Under Stress 42

Temperament..42

Emotional Markers 43

Productive Markers....................................43

Predisposition 43

Past Pointers 44

Personal Demons 44

Present Environment.................................45

Building Your Satan 45

20 Questions to Ask Your Character 46

Chapter 4

Been There, Scene That...49

Making A Scene 50

Action!..50

Background 50

Conflict...51

Decision 51

Scene Summary 51

Memorable Moments 52

Four Questions to Ask 52

Scene Elements...53

Failure is Good 53

When To Go Short 55
When To Go Long 55
Scene Placement 55
Sweet Spots 56
Pocket Suspense 56
Opening Your Scene 57
Action Scenes 58
Reaction Scenes 58
Setup Scenes 58
In Conclusion 59
Finally 59

Chapter 5

Writing Romantic Comedy 61
How to Write the Romantic Comedy 61
The Basic Romantic Comedy Plot 61
Opposites Attract 62
Begin with Larger Than Life Leads 62
Empathy for Your Characters 63
Readers Want Characters with Shared Goals and
Morals 63
Perseverance – Insurmountable Obstacles Must
Separate the Pair 64
Deception – The First Sin 64
Action and Overreaction 65
Character Motivation 65
Other Primary Characters 66
Inciting Incident 66
Call to Action, Denial, Repeat 67
1ˢᵗ Meeting: A Chance Encounter 67

2nd Meeting: Background Revealed, Values
Presented, Ground Rules Established 68
3rd Meeting: First Physical Encounter 68
4th Meeting: Falling for Each Other While in
Pursuit of External Goals 69
5th Meeting: Surprises at Work...................... 69
6th Meeting: First Fight.............................. 70
Secondary Characters 70
7th Meeting: Domestic Encounters................. 70
Point of No Return 71
8th Meeting: Goals Derailed 71
First Termination 72
Secondary Characters Strategize to Keep the
Couple Together...................................... 72
10th Meeting: Meet the Family 72
11th Meeting: Prom Night 73
Secrets Revealed 73
Final Termination 73
The Chase Scene 73
It's Too Late 74
12th Meeting: The Final Encounter 74
13th Meeting: Tying Up the Loose Ends 74

Chapter 6

WRITING THE COZY MYSTERY...75
How to Write the Cozy Mystery 75
What Is A Cozy Mystery?............................ 75
The Cozy Mystery Sleuth............................ 76
Show the Body.. 77
Introduce Your Sleuth 77

CONTENTS

Set the Scene 78

Reveal Clues 78

Introduce Subplot 78

Sell the Subplot to Your Reader 79

Send Your Sleuth Forward 79

Reveal Facts About Suspects 80

Raise Doubts About Each Suspect 80

Complicate the Case 81

Reveal Your Sleuth's Background 81

Kill Off Your Main Suspect 82

Raise the Stakes 82

Broaden the Investigation 83

Reveal Hidden Motives 83

Reflect Upon Earlier Clues 84

Stump Your Sleuth 84

Your Sleuth In Solitude 84

Sleuth Seeks Proof 85

Resolution of Subplot 85

The Climax 86

Resolution 86

Chapter 1

WHAT IS PLOT?

Plot is the answer to the question, "So...what happens in the story?" History is a series of events presented in chronological order. Your life is the history of one human. A story is a carefully crafted telling of events.

You do not have a story until something goes wrong.
~ STEVEN JAMES

When a reader selects your book they ask, "What's it about?" The premise of your story should offer conflict, a clearly defined Hero, intriguing bad guy, and a quest of a primeval goal. Maslow's hierarchy of needs suggest there are three primary human needs.

Safety: Security reflects your main character's need to protect his/her environment, health, or financial well-being.

Love: Affection is your Lead's need for friendship, intimacy, and family.

Esteem: A sense of self-worth reflects your Hero's primal need to be respected. Esteem presents our desire to be accepted and valued by others.

Paramount among these needs is our desire for survival, food, sex, the protection and sanctuary of loved ones, and our own fear of death.

Plot, and thus a great story, is a series of cleverly arranged events, the purpose of which is to tap into these primal needs and invoke an emotional response from the reader: Joy, hope, sorrow, laughter, fear, or anger. Your goal is to touch the soul of the reader.

The promise of the premise is encapsulated in the question, "What's it about?" This is the essence of your story and your "plot pitch." As you consider your story's premise, seek a single adjective that describes your Hero, an adjective for your bad guy, and a compelling goal to which the readers can relate. Your story's premise statement—summarized in your book's tagline and back-cover copy—hints at your Lead's journey. Who is he/she? Who is she fighting? What does he want and what are the stakes?

We remember characters; we pitch plot.

CONFLICT

Imagine a story without problems: The journey begins; the journey ends. Nice scenery, a few postcard moments, and one big yawn. Without trouble, conflict, and a crisis, there's no story and nothing to recall. How can you laugh about the bad times if there aren't any? Struggle is the substance of life. A story filled with character angst and torment pulls us in.

In our daily lives we go to great lengths to avoid conflict, but as writers, we love characters at odds with one another. Consider the popularity of today's reality TV shows. They're almost entirely based on one thing: conflict. Producers search for individuals who are in conflict with one another and throw them into competitive situations where jealousy and betrayal thrive.

It's the same with your story. You can create wonderful characters, but if they're talking about the weather or what they ate for breakfast, your readers will be asleep before they reach the bottom of the first page. Conflict is energy, and energy fuels your plot.

The only hard and fast rules are that you need both internal and external conflict. **Internal conflict** drives your character's emotional life. **External conflict** drives your story forward.

The "dark moment" is where internal and external conflict collide, crushing your Lead in the middle.

The three fundamental elements of storytelling are **character**, **plot,** and **conflict**. Plot and conflict are intertwined.

STORY SUMMARY

PORTRAIT: Show your Lead's normal life.
CRISIS: Show the great disturbance that disrupts his life.

The core of every story is about a character who wants something but cannot get it.
~ STEVEN JAMES

STRUGGLE: Your Lead tries to restore order to his life.

DISCOVER: Your Lead reaches a moment of realization.

CHANGE: Your Lead's life is transformed. Hint at the lesson he's learned.

PORTRAIT: Show your Lead's new normal life.

Your Lead should:
- Move forward toward a goal.
- Set his/her goals early in the story. (Hint: the reader needs to see where your Hero is along his journey.)
- Seek to satisfy an overarching want or need.
- Solve a problem.
- Be fully engaged in the story. Your story will fail if the Lead can just walk away from the problem.

If your Lead can walk away from the problem, the story fails because the reader is asking:
- What's the story about?
- Is anything happening?
- Why should I care what happens to these characters?

Your Lead's objective is the driving force of your story. It generates motion and keeps the Lead leaning forward. An objective can take two forms: To **GET** something or the **GET AWAY** from something. Solid plots have one and only one primary objective for the Lead.

POWER OF EXPERIENCE

What readers seek is an experience different from their own. Story is how readers dream. Story is what sells the book. The power of the premise is what captures the reader, editor, or agent's attention—not the characters and prose. Unless we care about the story we will never welcome the actors on stage. It is this power of desire that pulls us into the story.

Where will your story take your characters (emotionally, spiritually, physically, mentally, or relationally)? That's what readers want to know.
~ STEVEN JAMES

POWER OF DESIRE

- What does your Lead want?
- Why does he/she want it?
- Why can't she/he have it?
- How does your Lead go after what he wants?

Knowing *why* your Lead wants what he/she wants is the true source of motivation and the agent of change for your character.

WHO IS YOUR LEAD?

A strong plot begins with a compelling character; an interesting Lead. In the best plots, the Lead is someone we have to watch throughout the course of the novel, someone so real, distinctive and interesting that the reader is willing to forgo food and sleep to find out how his life ends. Who is the most likeable? The one we want to root for and see win. This is your Lead. What character offers the most conflict, longest jour-

Romance novels are not about romance but romantic tension.
~ STEVEN JAMES

ney, greatest growth, and biggest life change? What character learns the largest lesson? Who carries the theme of your story? Find that individual and you have your main character.

Your Lead's "likeability" is the primary reason we are drawn to the journey and the single most important element in pulling us into the story. Carefully consider the personal nature of your Lead. Blake Snyder, author of *Save the Cat*, argues there are only eight main character archetypes.

Young man on the rise (somewhat dim-witted, but tenacious: a character we want to see succeed)

Good girl tempted (pure of heart, cute and clever)

Bright and resourceful child (think *Home Alone*)

Sex goddess (calendar girl)

The hunk (calendar guy!)

Wounded soldier going back for a last redemptive mission (retired cop, washed up gunslinger, banished detective)

Troubled sex goddess (brilliant mind trapped in a gorgeous body)

Lovable fop (attractive and funny whose sensitivity and deep emotions remain hidden)

Court jester (hilariously funny)

Wise grandfather (sage)

CONFLICT = TENSION

Your Lead must be opposed by something—person, natural force, inner demons. Your story's main problem is the primary source of dramatic conflict. No hurdles, no conflict—no story. Con-

External struggles ignite reader interest and curiosity while internal and interpersonal struggles engender empathy.
~ STEVEN JAMES

flict moves the story forward and shapes your character. Opposition from characters and outside forces brings your story to life. Through your Lead's struggles he/she will grow or shrink but never remain the same.

INTERNAL AND EXTERNAL CONFLICT

Literary fiction is usually more about the inner life of your Lead. Commercial fiction is primarily about action—things happening to your Lead from the outside.

Inner vs. Outer

INNER: What does your Lead want to change about himself or herself?

OUTER: What does your Lead want that he/she thinks will bring happiness?

Your Lead needs to answer the questions: "Who do I want to be?" and "What do I want?"

Character Conflict

Character conflict focuses on your Lead's internal struggle. This obstacle prevents your Lead from progressing as a person. Conflict reveals your Lead's knowledge of what he/she thinks will make him/her happy. This quest is the internal motivation for your Lead.

Driven to Disrupt

Balance motivation against opposition. You need a strong protagonist and a stronger antagonist. Increase the energy level by foreshadowing challenges, raising the stakes of failure, and making the "hot water" hotter. Deliver short-range problems frequently to keep the reader off balance.

Problems = Energy

- Each scene must have a problem.

- Balance opposing forces so that your Lead and the villain are competitive.
- Increase the energy level by introducing more and larger problems.
- Foreshadow disaster.
- Raise the stakes of failure; make the hot water hotter.

Anything that interferes with the protagonist reaching her goal and fulfilling her unmet desire is the antagonist.
~ STEVEN JAMES

One overarching problem or want is not enough. Skilled writers add short-range problems and needs that help or hinder the success of the Lead. Keep your Lead in perpetual trouble and the reader will keep turning the page.

PACING AND PULSE

- Orchestrate short-range problems.
- Dribble them out and keep the reader uncertain as to their outcome.
- Adjust pacing by using short scenes with powerful outcomes.
- Use humor to give your reader a break from the tension. This prepares the reader for a new jolt of problems, pulling them forward through the story.

HOPE VS. FEAR

The writer creates a hope in the reader that the Lead will accomplish what he/she wants, but continually builds a fear that he/she will fail. This interaction of hope and fear produces tension.

Stories revolve around dilemmas, not action.
~ STEVEN JAMES

KNOCKOUT = SUCCESS

Readers love to slow down, rubberneck, and discuss the wreck they've just witnessed. They want to see worlds colliding and crashing, and characters losing their grip on hope. Your story's end should be unpredictable but inevitable. So begin with a great disturbance.

THE GREAT DISTURBANCE

What terrible or wonderful event enters the life of your Lead and disrupts his/her status quo, giving him a goal that will drive him through the story? It is this particular event that makes your story unique. How is the disturbance the best and worst thing that could happen to your Hero? What does your Hero need to learn? For your Lead, the catalyst is not what it seems. It's the opposite of good news. But it does lead to change and growth. This change is your reader's lesson and the theme of your story.

PLOT IN ACTION!

The basic structure of plot and the three-act framework are so universal that it is embedded in our DNA (We're born, we live, we die.) We accept the three-act structure because it echoes the structure of our days: We rise (to an adventure), work (through our problems), and we return (to somewhat of a normal home).

> *Giving the character what he longs for (or believes that he longs for) early in the story is a way to promise readers that things are going to go very wrong very soon.*
> ~ STEVEN JAMES

Act One: Familiar Surroundings Falling Apart

Every story opens with the introduction of your main character. Here the reader must have a clear sense of what the story is about. What is its tone, promise, the problem for its main characters, and the types of characters we will meet? Blake Snyder, author of *Save the Cat*, writes: "The Hero has to do something when we meet him so that we like him and want him to win." This single enduring quality will bond your readers to your main character.

Though problems exist for your main character, your Lead will remain in his/her normal world unless and until something throws everything off balance. This is your Lead's "inciting incident." This great disturbance shifts your Lead's life in a new direction. Many times your Lead will resist this call to action (presenting the seeds of inner conflict). In this debate section, your Lead must wrestle with a question. Here you will hint at the sacrifice to be made later. An additional element (prize or punishment) will be added to the mix and finally your Lead will accept the challenge and depart. Thus Act One will move from:

- Introduction
- Inciting Incident / Great Disturbance
- Call to Action / Denial of Call / Acceptance of Call to Action
- Identification of Your Lead's Goal
- Advance

The curtain comes down, marking the end of the first act. In order to move your Lead from Act One into Act Two, he/she must pass through what James Scott Bell calls a "one way door." If your lead can return to his/her previous life, then he/she hasn't jettisoned his/her old life for the new.

> *To initiate your story, your protagonist will either (1) lose something vital and try to regain it, (2) see something desirable and try to obtain it, or (3) experience something traumatic and try to overcome it.*
> ~ STEVEN JAMES

Act Two: Problems, People, and Growth

Act Two reveals your Lead's emotional journey as he/she overcomes obstacles. As the hurdles become more frequent and larger, you raise the stakes for your Lead. Both inner and outer struggles will mark your Lead's journey as they move toward what appears to be certain defeat. Include both reversals of fortune and unexpected blessings to give your reader both a sense of hope and dread.

Early in Act Two, change your Lead's status. Depending on your Lead's "normal" life, *remove* or *increase* your Lead's power, position, and prestige. Oftentimes your character becomes the opposite of what he was in Act One. Think Harry Potter. At the beginning of each book, Harry is in Muggleland, without power, prominence, or freedom. In Act Two (at Hogwarts), Harry finds himself powerful, revered, and favored by the faculty.

Act Two will consume the major part of your story. Often called the "muddle," the bulk of your action takes place here. Regardless of whether the conflict is internal or external, your lead must face a series of confrontations, both small and large, between him/her and the opposition. Act Two moves from:

- Small Hurdles
- Status Change
- Fun & Games
- Large Hurdles, Death, Danger, & Conflict
- Black Moment
- Glimmer of Hope

Act Two is an inverted mirror of your Lead's normal world in Act One. Here, the characters from Act One appear as enlarged or diminished personalities. For example, in the Harry Potter stories, the character of Dudley Dursley (Harry's antagonistic, spoiled, and *bungling* stepbrother) appears in Act Two as the

Three types of struggles all interweave in stories and create different types of reader engagement and reaction: internal struggles (a question that needs to be answered), external struggles (a problem that needs to be solved), and interpersonal struggles (relationships that need to be started or restored)
~ STEVEN JAMES

antagonistic, spoiled, and *powerful* Draco Malfoy. (They even share the same first letter in their first name.) The first half of Act Two is the fun and games portion of the story. This often coincides with your character's "status change." (Again, the idea of "status change" is to flip your Lead's position, power, or prestige. If they're rich in Act One, they become poor in Act Two. Single in Act One? In love in Act Two. Unemployed in Act One? CEO of the company in Act Two.) Here in the fun and games scenes, your main characters bond, travel, explore, and learn about each other. Often the tone is light and painted in rich colors.

Midway through Act Two your Lead will reach a high or low point reflecting a turn in his/her journey. The midpoint is never as good as it seems or as bad as we fear, but it does mark "halftime" for your Lead's journey. Now the stakes are raised. The bad guys become worse. The danger increases. There is a hint of death and your Lead faces conflict at every turn. Each scene brings him/her closer to the "black moment"—the instance where all appears lost.

To move from Act Two to Act Three, your lead must reach a breaking point. This is your Lead's moment of crisis: his/her crucifixion. Here the story will demand that a principle or person be sacrificed for the good of the goal. This is the point where your Hero's old world and old way of thinking die to the "new normal." With nothing left to lose, your Lead is willing to risk everything for one last shot at reaching the goal. Once committed, your Lead can't go back. He/she rushes through another one-way door.

The heart of a story is tension, desire, crisis, escalation, struggle, discovery, and transformation.
~ STEVEN JAMES

But before you rush into Act Three, ask: Where is my tender romance scene? Where is my sacrifice scene? Where is my Lead's disappointment scene? Where is my scary scene? Where is my funny scene? If you cannot find these scenes in your story, make a note to go back and add them later. These scenes will add richness and texture to your story.

Act Three

Thrust into another new world, your Lead faces his/her greatest fear: the one thing they hoped would never happen. This shift in direction is the second great transition. Any form of transpiration will work. The idea is to allow your reader to *see* your character moving toward the final confrontation. Thus, in Act Three your Lead will experience:

- Transition
- Walk to the Cross
- Win or Lose
- Climax

A mode of transportation will deposit your Lead at the edge of their internal and external battlefield. From here they will walk to his/her cross with the outcome of their journey in question. Upon reaching the summit, your Lead will face his/her final confrontation. He/she will either reach the goal or fail miserably. After the dust settles, tie up the loose ends. The ending of your novel will tell the reader how to feel and what to think about the events that just happened.

EXAMPLE OF PLOT IN ACTION

Act One

Introduction: The youngest son of a wealthy man feels oppressed by his overbearing older brother.

Inciting Incident/Great Disturbance: On his twenty-first birthday he visits the bank and withdraws all the money from his trust fund.

Call to Action: Sensing a chance to break away from his father and the family business, the boy decides to leave home.

Identification of Your Lead's Goal: Packing his bags, he plots his new life.

Advance: The boy sets out for Las Vegas.

Act Two
Fun & Games. The boy runs with a fast crowd.

Small Hurdles. He soon loses all his money to gambling, women, drugs, and drink.

Status Change. Out of money and on the street, the son of a wealthy father finds himself bankrupt, friendless, and homeless.

Large Hurdles, Death, Danger, & Conflict. Destitute, lacking skills and street smarts, the young man applies for any job he can, but is turned away each time. (If this sounds like your life as a writer, keep reading!)

Black Moment. The boy settles for the lowest job in the city—scrubbing toilets in the MGM casino.

Glimmer of Hope: Having hit bottom, the young man decides to go home. Maybe he can get a job working in his dad's warehouse.

Act Three
Transition. The scene opens with your Lead stepping from the rig of an eighteen-wheeler.

Walk to the Cross. As the truck pulls away, your Lead starts up a darkened road.

Win or Lose. An expensive car speeds past. Moments later, brake lights flash; the car stops.

Climax. The boy sees his father exiting the car. They make eye contact. His father reaches for the door handle as if to get back in the car and then...grabbing his jacket from the front seat...the father runs to the young man. They hug. The father puts his coat on his son.

Tie up loose ends. The father tells his son to wash up; they're going to the club to celebrate. But the older son refuses to join them. Over dinner the younger son is given a high position in his dad's company while the older son sits home fuming, thus presenting the conflict for the sequel.

Chapter 2

DRAMATIC DIALOGUE

Ascene is: **Doing (Action), Thinking (Narrative), and Talking (Dialogue)**

Obviously, we can't know what others are thinking. We can see them moving, doing, and we find that interesting. But when they speak, we listen. The cell phone rings and we answer it. A loud speaker blares and we pause. Talk is not cheap. Talk is tension.

A writer has a number of tools for story building: **narration**, **action**, **description**, and **dialogue**.

Description and narration will move it slowly, steadily, and easily along. Think literature.

Action and dialogue will speed it along—dialogue more so than action. *When characters start talking, the story starts walking.*

Dialogue reveals theme. "Sometimes the right course demands an act of piracy." In the movie *Pirates of the Caribbean*, Jack Sparrow actually states the theme of the story in dialogue. When possible, allow your main character to speak the theme through dialogue.

FUNCTION OF DIALOGUE

Dialogue reveals the character's motives and opposing agendas. A dialogue scene propels the story into high gear. We love to eavesdrop; through words we reveal our heart. We introduce our characters through dialogue, expose their motivation, wants and needs.

Behavior is external; motives are internal. Dialogue presents both at once.

ELEMENTS OF DIALOGUE

For dialogue to work it must:
1. Sound right for each character. There are four aspects to consider:
   - Vocabulary (words each character uses)
   - Words & Expressions unique to each character (establish a saying or phrase early in the story)
   - Regionalism
   - Dialect (accent)
2. Since dialogue is best when it is an extension of action, give your characters different agendas in a scene. Then the dialogue will take care of itself.

REFLECTIVE DIALOGUE

Reflective dialogue allows the characters to interpret a previous conversation with introspective thoughts. With reflective dialogue, what's said matters less than the thoughts and emotions of the character as they think about the conversation.

EXAMPLE: "Then I said, 'No, I won't have it ready. Not when you want it.' That's what I told him. My life was a mess. I'm behind in everything, the reports pile up faster than I can get them out and does he care? No. He just keeps piling on the work. As if I don't have enough to do already with the merger and the staff reductions. Hey, have you heard anything I've said?" (*Writing Dialogue as Memorable Voices*)

MISDIRECTED DIALOGUE

Here one character seeks to have a direct conversation while the other evades and dances away. Ironically, the lack of response is a sign of intimacy. Misdirected dialogue is the type of conversation that most naturally takes advantage of the rhythms and cadences of language. Here, the natural tendency is to leave tensions hanging, rather than rush toward resolution.

With misdirected dialogue you:
- Change the subject.
- Direct the dialogue offstage (to another party).
- Answer questions with answers that aren't quite answers but sound like them.
- Allow characters to speak to themselves out loud.
- Carry on more than one conversation at the same time.

EXAMPLE: "I need a beer. Could I have a beer?"

"I saw Mary today."

"Beer, please."

"She was getting her nails done."

"Natural Lite. Anything for you?"

"Beer gives me a headache."

"Bottle, no glass." He turned back toward her. "I wasn't suggesting you get tanked. God, you're so—"

"What?"

"How'd Mary look? Bet she looked hot. She still tanned?"

"Maybe I'll order a beer after all."

"I need a beer. Could I have a beer?" *(directing the dialogue offstage to the waiter)*

"I saw Mary today." *(changing the subject)*

"Beer, please."

"She was getting her nails done."

"Natural Lite. Anything for you?"

"Beer gives me a headache." *(answering questions with answers that aren't really answers but sound like them)*

"Bottle, no glass." He turned back toward her. "I wasn't suggesting you get tanked. God, you're so..." *(allowing characters to speak to themselves out loud)*

"What?"

"How'd Mary look? Bet she looked hot. She still tanned?" *(changing the subject)*

"Maybe I'll order a beer after all." *(changing the subject)*

(Writing Dialogue by Tom Chiarella)

MODULATED DIALOGUE

Modulated dialogue provides introspection and irony. Here the emphasis isn't on the interpretation of the conversation but on the collision of details presented by the narrative. Your characters comment on what's said and why. Each piece of dialogue becomes a portal for the character to swerve into a memory or opinion.

EXAMPLE: "You bought a truck?" *What was it with guys and trucks?*

"Guess what I paid for it?"

"I couldn't begin to."

"Try. Take a wild guess."

"A million dollars."

"Twenty-two thousand."

"Really?" *My college tuition cost less. Of course I received scholarship money.*

"Got it for three grand less than Blue Book value."

"Is that a good deal?" *How could buying a truck ever be a good deal?*

"Are you crazy?"

I must be. How else do you explain me talking to you. "Did you trade in the KIA?"

"Nope. Financing it. Wouldn't give me what it was worth."

No surprise there. Everything about this guy is overvalued. "Can I buy it?"

"The KIA? Why? You know I'll take you anyplace you want to go."

Doubt it. Not in a truck. Not in a KIA. Not in my lifetime.

BREATHLESS DIALOGUE

Breathless dialogue is the opposite of descriptive dialogue. Here cut away most of the expository narrative in order to increase the tempo of the dialogue. Insert bits of action to keep the scene moving forward in a physical way. Use short spurts of emotional phrases. Make clear what's at stake for the reader. A good way to do this is to compress your dialogue.

Compressing Dialogue

Dialogue fails when it swells. To remove bloated dialogue, compress the conversation. Restrict responses to three to five words.

"You mean it? Five words?"

"Or less."

"Can't be done."

"You just did."

"But it's not natural."

"'Course it is."

"What about introspection, emotion, and_"

"Adverbs and adjectives. Ditch 'em."

"But they're so…"

"Unnecessary. Cut the fat."

"Five words."

"Or less."

Remember, interruption adds tension. Allow your characters to interrupt each other, to complete sentences, and to repeat each other's words or phrasing. When struggling with the five-word rule, allow a character to change the subject, to interrupt the other speaker, or to echo a word.

I Have Rhythm

With rhythm dialogue you think in terms of beats. The reader's ear hears the cadence while the eye communicates the information to the brain.

"I'll drive."

"You're too drunk."

"Not yet."

"Yes, you are."

"And you're not?"

"Just one." She reached for the keys. "Give 'em to me."

"No way."

Not only does this type of dialogue present conflict and tension but it also uses a three beat, two beat cadence that adds a musical quality to the narrative. You wouldn't want to drag this out, but for short bursts where you want to create the undertone of a particular mood, rhythm dialogue works in the absence of a musical score.

CIRCLE BACK

Another way to add tension to dialogue is to circle back to a word or phrase spoken earlier by another character.

"I saw Dave outside McDonald's last night. He was so wasted."

"Like that's new."

"Can't you speak to him?"

"Me? Why me?"

"Because you of all people know how destructive binge drinking can be."

"He's not going to listen to me."

"Have you tried?"

"Wait? Outside McDonald's? Aren't you under house arrest?"

"I snuck out."

In this scene the first speaker passes judgment on both Dave and the second speaker. We don't learn of the first speaker's flaws until the conversation circles back to the McDonald's comment.

THE SILENT TREATMENT

Studies show that most of our communication is non-verbal so let your characters sulk, shrug, and stew in silence.

Silencing a character allows them to answer dialogue with action, not words. No response is often the best response. By shifting the focus at the moment we most expect to hear the character speak, we interject surprise and tension. With the silent answer, the conversation continues through gestures.

Let's look at three types of silent gestures.

DRAMATIC GESTURE

A dramatic gesture reinforces the narrative exchange. Stubbing out a cigarette might mark the end of a conversation… and relationship.

When your character shoves his hands in his pocket, he may be telling the others that he's pulling back, closing off, and refusing to divulge more information.

When is the right time for a dramatic gesture? When the dialogue between two characters threatens to drag on and you want to leave tension in the air. Rather than have your character respond, simply let them act out their answer. The abrupt exit and slamming of a door is cliché, but it does send a message to the reader.

UNIQUE GESTURE

A unique gesture is a specific trait of your character. These are the tip-offs we give to others, often unconsciously. A woman touches the top button of her blouse before she speaks. She leans towards a man to whom she's attracted. She holds eye contact. She may play with her hair, sending an unconscious signal that she wishes to be stroked in a similar way.

To create intimacy or tension, show your character's unique gestures. Often our silence says volumes.

INCIDENTAL GESTURE

The incidental gesture expands the scope of the conversation, drawing the props and setting them into the dialogue. A widower swats gnats at a funeral, a small boy plugs his ears as the ambulance races past, a young woman taps her foot to a bar room song. Incidental gestures can suggest that one character is disengaged from the conversation, thus adding... tension.

DIRECTED DIALOGUE

Writing dialogue is about energy and direction. Tone and emotion provide the energy for the story. Direction gives it tension. Writers develop an ear for dialogue. They listen, repeat and cut. Here are four ways to structure dialogue.

Directed dialogue ratchets up the story's tension. Through directed dialogue your characters remind the reader just how desperate they are to achieve their goals. As your hero becomes more desperate, his adversary grows certain of success; the reader knows this because of the confident tone in the voice of the antagonist.

Idiom – Use abbreviations, slang, and acronyms. "FYI, MO, OMG! AWOL

Reversals – rebuts a directed comment and is noted by its sarcasm, challenging, or chiding tone.

Shifts in pace – Drop tags to speed up pace; add them to slow it down

Shift in tone – Add glib comments to shift from formal to informal talk

Interruption – Cut off one speaker

Silences – Represented by dead air, no response.

Echoing – One speaker repeats another's comment.

PARENT, ADULT, CHILD

The parent is the seat of authority, the one with power. P lays down the law.

The adult is the most objective, rational, and even-tempered. A will often say, "Let's be adults about this."

The child is irrational, emotional, and selfish. C wants what he wants when he wants it.

In any scene at least two roles will evolve. During the course of the conversation the two characters will often switch roles in order to achieve their agenda.

Think "rock, paper, scissors" but with words.

DO'S AND DON'T S OF TAGS

When it comes to tags, stick with he said, she said. Never lose faith in the word "said."

Yes, it is overused but for the reader the tag "he said" is an afterthought.

No Tags: Skip tags and frame your characters' words with snippets of description, thought, or action.

"Fine, I'll drive. You hold the snake." Pam cut her eyes toward the box in Dan's lap. The cardboard lid lifted a few inches. "And would you stop pointing that gun out the window?"

You can also skip tags for short stretches provided you reintroduce the character every few lines. After six to eight lines of back-and-forth dialogue, however, you should tag a character so the reader doesn't loose track of who's speaking.

Tag Placement: Vary the placement for tags. The normal place for a tag is at the end: "...," he said.

You can also place a tag in the middle of the sentence to add emphasis. "I'd like another beer," Jane said, "in a bottle, no glass, and if it's not too much trouble, cold this time."

To add variety to your dialogue place a tag in the front: Jane said, "...

No Adverbs: Avoid adverbs and exclamation points. If you're tempted to write, *"come here," she said, lovingly,* don't. Drop the adverb and show her leaning toward him, kicking off her shoes, and rubbing her bare foot on the back of his leg.

Any Participles Present? One present participle is fine—two sprinkled through a conversation, acceptable. But don't over do it. Use a present participle to re-tag the character, but don't allow it to take away from the tension of the conversation.

EXAMPLE: "Fine, I'll drive," Pam said, sliding behind the wheel. "You hold the snake."

"Why you? How come I can't drive?" Dan asked, tossing the shoe box on the passenger floor board.

"Ah, hello? You're bleeding." Reaching down she pressed the lid back on the box, then added, "Besides, you can't drive a stick."

PUNCTUATION

Punctuation goes inside the quotes. "… It's that simple," he said.

Period goes at the end of the sentence, like so, "… It's that simple," he said.

Question marks and your one exclamation mark go inside quotes. "Seriously? You think it's that simple?" she asked.

When using a punctuation mark inside quotes do not add a comma. Incorrect. "…You think it's that simple?," she asked.

When someone new speaks, begin a new paragraph.

When one character speaks for a long time you can skip the closing quote mark, but you must begin the new paragraph with a quote mark.

"…yada yada yada yada yada yada yada yada.

"More yada yada yada yada.

Use italics for emphasis and to show a character's thoughts. *Oh, and it's not like you've ever been wrong.* Just don't do this too often; otherwise you yank the reader out of the fictional dream. *Am I being clear; do they get it? Or should I give them more examples. No, one is enough.*

Use ellipses for words in a character's speech that trail off…

Use a dash to show an interruption or character who breaks off in the middle of—

Use contractions if they suit your character. There are exceptions, however. Even if your character normally uses contractions, there comes a time when they say words slowly to emphasize something important… usually a lie.

Under oath, if someone doesn't use a contraction when answering a question, then they're probably lying.

"I did not have sex with that woman—Ms. Lewinsky."

"I did not, could not, would not kill Nicole."

7 Essentials for Dialogue

1. Is the narrative essential to the story? Does it provide necessary information, extend the action, or advance the character's agenda? Does it reveal a character flaw or asset? Does it reinforce the theme of the story?
2. Does it flow naturally from the character's mouth?
3. Does it contain conflict and add tension? (NO CHIT CHATS ALLOWED)
4. Does it sound right for the story, setting, time period, and geography?
5. Does it sound right for the character that is speaking?
6. Does it sound like real speech minus the *ums, ahs* and *huhs*?
7. Can the dialogue be compressed?

Chapter 3

CREATING COMPELLING CHARACTERS

What makes a character compelling? Simple. Something happens to them. Even if you despise your (_____), you enjoy telling others about his failures. "Did you hear what happened to my ex? He got busted for…" We love to loath, meddle in the affairs of others, and watch them fail. Our participation in their lives expands our world, which explains part of what fuels reality TV.

CHARACTERS MUST…

- Reveal heart
- Face obstacles
- Pick paths
- Make a discovery
- Reveal a secret

- Conquer a mountain

Building Characters

For your characters to be likable they should be witty, charming, wise, friendly, empathetic, authentic, encouraging, secure, or vulnerable.

If your lead is perfect she's boring, so give her both redeeming qualities and flaws so the reader can relate.

Goals for Your Lead

- What does she want?
- What is she willing to do to reach her goal?
- What WILL she do to reach that goal?
- What is she willing to sacrifice?
- What happens if the she fails?
- Is your Lead larger than life?
  (Does he lay in the middle of highway, hang from a Ferris wheel, and rebuild an old house for the girl he loves?)

Want, Need, Motivation

If the reader questions why a character reacts in a certain way, then you've lost credibility. There are two reasons your characters act "out of character."

1. There is no clear motivation for the character to perform the action.
2. The motivation provided isn't sufficiently developed.

THE JOURNEY OF YOUR LEAD

- What decision must your Lead make? (Act 1)
- What does your lead learn during the decision-making process? (Act 2 / 3)
- How does her decision reveal who she is? (Act 2)
- How does her decision impact the other characters in the story? (Act 2)
- What does she lose as a result of her decision? (Act 2 / 3)
- What does she gain from her decision? (Act 3)

DEPTH OF YOUR LEAD

Start with what's wrong. Character depth begins with the flaws, but true character development is found in the reason for the flaws. The motivation is where the suspense resides, and the more your Lead's motivation mirrors that of your reader then the greater the bond.

S T R E T C H YOUR LEAD

Novelist Susan May Warren suggests you stretch your Lead by asking:

"What is your Lead's greatest fear? (abandonment, for example) Make that fear come true in your story. Identify your Lead's security blanket, that place where they feel safe. Then yank it away. What are your Lead's hot

buttons, those things that set her off? Make your Lead answer the question, "Who Am I?" in dialogue. Show your Lead's "let me do it!" scene: their competency skill. Where is your Lead's zone? That place of control and swagger. Does your Lead have a spiritual place? Take them there. Show your character wanting to quit. Make them say, 'I quit!' Define at least two rock-solid beliefs for your Lead: For example: Loyalty to others & Honesty. Then pit those two beliefs against each other.

CONSEQUENCES FOR YOUR LEAD

As your story unfolds, raise the stakes so that your Lead's success or failure impacts not just:
- Him / Her but… (Act 2, scene 3)
- Family (Act 2, scene 5)
- Community (Act 2, scene 7)
- World (Act 2, scene 9)

This is the "ripple effect."

CREATIVE TRUST

Novelist John D. MacDonald encourages authors to invite readers into a contract of creative trust. (*The Writer's Handbook, 50*[th] *Anniversary Edition* by Sylvia K. Burack)

"The writer is like a person trying to entertain a listless child on a rainy afternoon. You set up a card table and lay out pieces of cardboard, construction paper, scissors, paste, crayons. You draw a rectangle and you construct a very colorful little fowl and stick it in the foreground, and you say, "This is a chicken." You cut out a red square and put it in the background and you say, "This is a barn." You construct a bright yellow truck and put it in the background on the other side of the frame and say, 'This is a speeding truck. Is the chicken going to get out of the way in time? Now you finish the picture.'

Internal and interpersonal struggles create reader empathy and an emotional connection with the story, while external struggles create curiosity.
~ STEVEN JAMES

"The child becomes involved, adding trees, a fence, a roof on the barn. You didn't say anything about trees, cows and fences. But he (and the reader) puts them in because they know these are the furniture of farms. They join in the creative act. Or not. How can you lose your child, your reader? By putting in too much detail, turning the reader into a spectator.

"You can also lose your reader by not adding enough detail to your Lead. Each character should have a presence. The chicken, not a chicken. He is eleven weeks old. He is a rooster named Melvin who stands proud and glossy in the sunlight, but tends to be nervous, insecure and hesitant. His legs are exceptionally long, and in full flight he has a stride you wouldn't believe.

"He's a rooster named Melvin who stands proud (internal asset or flaw?) and glossy (attractive appearance) in the sunlight, but tends to be nervous, insecure and hesitant (why, we wonder). His legs are long (physically fit), and in full flight he has a stride you wouldn't believe (hint of superior power)."

(*The Writer's Handbook, 50th Anniversary Edition* by Sylvia K. Burack)

PULLING FOR THE HERO

Climax: What's a moral dilemma my hero might face?
~ STEVEN JAMES

In these few sentences have you found yourself pulling for Melvin, wanting to see him escape the speeding truck? Perhaps you can identify with Melvin's nervous, pigeon-toed walk (Melvin's a mixed-breed bird). Were you inspired by his willingness to extend himself to run flat out? The point is the reader now cares about Melvin.

CARE COMES FIRST

For your reader to become engaged in the story, they must CARE about your characters.

"If a vague gray truck hits a vague gray man, his blood on gray pavement will be without color or meaning. Make your characters real. When a real yellow truck hits Melvin, we feel the mortal thud deep in that place that hints at our own impending death."

- John D. MacDonald

How to Make the Reader Care

Use short, vivid strokes. Take out subjective words. Don't label (no adverbs or adjectives). Tell how a man looks, not your evaluation of who he is. Don't say a man looks seedy. That's your opinion. Describe a pair of glasses mended with duct tape, tufts of hair growing out of his nostrils, a sour odor of sweat. Now we know this man. We've seen him on street corners, in the park, and at exit ramps holding a cardboard sign that reads, "will write for food."

> *Is there a moment of discovery about the world or about your protagonist that transforms his situation?*
> ~ STEVEN JAMES

Making a Character

There are four areas that shape your character.
- Predisposition
- Past
- Personal demons
- Present environment

Predisposition

Predisposition is the auto-mechanism that guides your character at the start of her journey. Her habits, manner of dress, quirks, and social interaction shape her in a way that is uniquely suited for her role in your story. Study her. Watch the way her hands swing when she walks, the shift in her eyes when confronted by her boss, and the way she twirls her hair whenever he walks in the room. Identify these traits and show them to the reader.

AT REST UNDER STRESS

How does your character appear at rest? Is she relaxed or does she fidget? Pace or slump? List five character-istics that describe her at rest. Next list five attributes that show how she reacts to stress. Does she curse, cry, vent, sweat profusely, or pout? What does she do with her hands; how does her breathing change?

TEMPERAMENT

The character you introduce first is a promise to readers. If you introduce a point-of-view character and then kill her off in the prologue, readers won't be as emotionally invested in the story.
~ STEVEN JAMES

Temperament is a person's manner of behaving, think-ing, and reacting to others and circumstances. Tempera-ment reveals itself best during stressful events, so after you define your character's ba-sic temperament, then turn up the heat and burn away the dross, the impurities. Al-low the reader to watch her change during the story.

EMOTIONAL MARKERS

Around others is she...
- Popular – appealing, talkative, cheerful, curious, expressive, good-humored?
- Powerful – dynamic, active, confidant, persistent, calm, compulsive, courageous?
- Thoughtful – thoughtful, artistic, idealistic, scatterbrained?

PRODUCTIVE MARKERS

At work is she...
- Popular – Energetic, willing to volunteer, patient, empathetic, witty?
- Powerful – Goal oriented, organized, team player, encouraging, perfectionist?
- Thoughtful – Detail oriented, tidy, prone to making charts, gets lost in the process?

PREDISPOSITION

What are her faults? Is she compulsive, prone to exaggerate, egotistical, hot-tempered, bossy, impatient, moody, a victim, shy, self-righteous, indecisive, combative? Define her flaws and expose them during the telling of the story.

Your protagonist becomes interesting when he becomes vulnerable.
~ STEVEN JAMES

PAST POINTERS

How was your character raised? What events shaped her? Dig into her past and reveal in small bites. Each element should reinforce why she acts, thinks, and feels the way she does.

Often one defining moment in her past is enough. Be selective, show her wounds, allow readers to touch her scar. Then ask:

- With what has she struggled? A physical affliction? Emotional wound?
- What has she discovered about herself?
- How has she changed over the years?

PERSONAL DEMONS

When you discover your protagonist's unmet desire, you find the essence of your story.
~ STEVEN JAMES

Internal conflict is the energy of your character. Imagine an angel on one shoulder and a devil on the other, each whispering into your Lead's ear. Allow the reader to see this internal struggle as your Lead weighs the consequences of her actions. It is here in the moral struggle between good and evil that your character will grow or shrink.

Every character must go through an internal transformation.

External struggles are problems that need to be solved.

Internal struggles are questions that need to be answered.

As your character solves the external problem, she gains insight into how to answer the inner questions.

To create a story with depth, get to know what she wants. Then reveal her motives by showing how she:

- Interacts with other characters
- Responds to events in the story
- Pursues her objective

PRESENT ENVIRONMENT

It's not the "what" that's important but the "why." Reveal her internal motivation for the way she dresses, talks, and acts.

Your job is to help the reader grasp the desires, motives, beliefs, attitudes, dreams, and frustrations of your characters.

Subtlety is key. Err on the side of understatement. The more you tell readers how to feel, the less they will.

Show emotion through action, dialogue, and body language.

The more personal the struggle and impending danger, the more suspenseful the story.

BUILDING YOUR SATAN

For your bad girl to be likable, she should have at least one of these qualities and the more she exhibits it, the

'he tension between your protagonist and an-
Ve want to pull for the bad girl because often
_ uur faults in others. We just don't want them
to win.

20 QUESTIONS TO ASK YOUR CHARACTER

1. Pretend you are walking down the street and you see your Lead for the first time. What word or phrase leaps to mind?

2. Describe the general physical impression presented by your character. Don't fuss over the exact phrasing. That will come later. For now you just want to be able to say, "He's about... with... and has a ... when he walks." Does the man on the sidewalk in front of your house remind you of an animal or object? Does his face have the shape of a weasel? When he walks, does he swing his arms in such a way as to imply that he's swimming in air? Does he remind you of a gazelle or goat?

3. Can you sense a color in your character, something beyond skin color or purely physical features? Does she smell of cinnamon or strawberries? When the wind blows, does her hair remind you of wheat fields?

4. What kinds of clothes does your character wear? This is an important key to her psyche. We can make modifications to our outward appearance, but it's much easier to change our look through the style of clothes we wear. Her wardrobe tells us a lot about who she thinks she is.

5. Can you describe her voice? Is it soothing or abrasive, enthusiastic or flat and dreary? Does your character speak with an accent, a lisp? How does she use words? Do they tumble out all at once or does she speak in a measured tone?

6. When was she born? Where did she live when she was growing up?

7. What were her earliest and most important influences?

8. Does she accept the standards of her day or does she rebel?

9. What is most important to her? What does she want more than anything else?

10. What is her conflict? Is it imposed upon her by circumstances, or did she bring trouble upon herself?

11. What does your character fear the most?

12. How does she handle competition, defeat, and loss?

13. How does she react to children, animals, foreigners, and old people?

Characters make choices to resolve tension.
~ STEVEN JAMES

14. Why would the character react the way she does? Forget the clichés and predictable patterns. Ask yourself how "your" character would react.

15. Does the character know why she behaves the way she does, or is there a subconscious motivation at work?

16. There are two motivations for actions. The thing the character believes in and the goal of which she's unaware. Often our actions betray our words.

When we allow the reader to see the transparency of a character, then the reader feels superior and cares more. Ask: What is it she wants?

17. What does she need?
18. What is your Lead's most undesirable and negative quality? Does this flaw bother her or does she expect others to adjust to her?
19. In your story will she change or become hardened by the circumstances you bring upon her?
20. Can you spend the next year living with this character?

Answer all these questions and you will know your characters—and so will your readers.

Chapter 4

BEEN THERE, SCENE THAT

WHAT IS A SCENE? The power of a scene is derived from the slightly claustrophobic feeling you get when you focus on the characters. They seem somehow trapped in a place, unable to leave. They are forced to face a main issue in the scene. Through your writing you pan across the scene and set the context, then move in for a close-up shot of the characters struggling. In order to engage the reader's imagination, your scenes must do one or more of the following:

Move the story through action
- Characterize through reaction
- Set up essential scenes to come
- Sprinkle in spice

A GOOD SCENE

- Reveals information that moves the story forward with new goals, old secrets, and hidden motives
- Shows conflict between characters (this adds tension)
- Deepens the character's development
- Creates suspense (introduces a new wrinkle that leaves the reader hanging)

MAKING A SCENE

Making a scene is as easy as: **ABCD A**ction **B**ackground **C**onflict **D**ecision

ACTION!

Static settings will put your readers to sleep, so get your characters moving. Show the world around them spinning. It can be something as simple as snow falling on a patio railing or bullets piercing the sides of the limo, but you must show movement. Make sure the reader "sees" something is happening.

BACKGROUND

Open with action, then place the scene in context. Why are the characters in the scene? How did they arrive? What does your Lead want? Background IS NOT history. Background IS showing your Lead's goal for that scene. Your character must want something. What is it? This is where you will state your Lead's goal for *this* scene.

In each scene ask "what is discovered?"
~ STEVEN JAMES

CONFLICT

Who or what stands in the way of your Lead reaching his goal? Present the barrier. Include conflict on every page. Never let your Lead relax. Show the struggle! Increase the risk of failure. Tension comes from unresolved conflict, so let the scene devolve into a mess.

DECISION

At the end of each scene, your Lead must choose. A scene moves from struggle, discovery, choice, and change. "Choice, not circumstances, dictate the direction of the story." -**Steven James**. In each scene your Lead must find a clue or open door to thrust her forward. PRESENT TWO PATHS AND MAKE YOUR LEAD PICK ONE!

SCENE SUMMARY

When you finish writing a scene, ask, "Is this scene necessary?" Read the scenes before and after. Does what just happened deserve its own scene? Could the information be placed in a neighboring scene?

MEMORABLE MOMENTS

What makes a scene memorable? The thing that catches the reader off guard. The emotion that transcends the page and speaks to the reader's heart. "Think of each memorable scene as an inner tube designed to keep the larger story afloat. The more memorable scenes there are, the more we see the entire story floating in front of us and the more we appreciate the whole work." – **Raymond Obstfeld**

A scene is memorable because it catches the reader looking the other way. The reader begins each scene with an expectation of what's about to happen, what will be delivered. Then you jerk the rug from beneath them with a new twist. How do you deliver a memorable scene? With surprise, suspense, deep emotion, or death.

At the conclusion of your story, go back and insert (at least) three memorable scenes that will stand out. Scenes that are so powerful and poignant that readers will rush to tell their friends. Think of the ending of *Casablanca*, Scarlet O'Hara with her fist raised to the darkened sky in *Gone with the Wind*, or ET with his alien finger extended, reaching for fellowship. Memorable scenes can sometimes carry an otherwise weak story.

FOUR QUESTIONS TO ASK

1. What is the purpose of the scene?
2. How should the reader feel after the scene?
3. What should the reader think after the scene?

4. What should the reader wonder after the scene?

SCENE ELEMENTS

- State the goal of your Lead
- "Promise pain" - Steven James
- "Deliver pain" - Steven James
- Progress from goal to conflict, disaster, character development
- Suspense is anticipation so announce the reward early in the scene
- Restate your Lead's goal as necessary
- Never let your Lead relax
- Increase the risk of failure
- Tension comes from unresolved conflict so leave your character's world messy
- "Suspense happens between the promise and the payoff so state the promise, then delay the payoff." - Steven James

FAILURE IS GOOD

To build energy into your story, allow your Lead to "fail her way to success. In each scene she WILL NOT get what she wants. She will get something else, instead." - Steven James. At the end of each scene, allow your Lead to process the action and make a decision that

Everything that happens in a story will be caused by the thing that precedes it.
~ STEVEN JAMES

The end of every scene must not only be logical but, in retrospect, the only possible conclusion to that scene. Scenes will end in a way that's unexpected and yet satisfying to readers.
~ STEVEN JAMES

pushes her forward. In this way your reader also thinks about what just happened and where the story is going.

GOAL: What does your Lead want at the beginning of the Scene? The Goal must be specific and it must be clearly defined. The reason your Lead must have a Goal is that it forces her to move. Your character is going after something she wants. Once the goal is set the reader can track the scene's progress and answer the question, "Are we getting close?"

CONFLICT: Conflict is the series of obstacles your Lead faces on the way to reaching his Goal. If your Lead reaches his Goal with no Conflict, then the reader is bored. Your reader wants to see struggle! No victory has any value if it comes too easily. So make your Lead struggle and your reader will live out their struggle.

DISASTER: For you, as the writer, a disaster is allowing your Lead to reach her goal. Don't let her! When a Scene ends in victory, your reader has no reason to turn the page. If things are going well, your reader might as well go to bed. Allow your Lead to "fail forward." She'll get something but not what she wanted.

Finish the scene by showing your Lead moving down her new path.

WHEN TO GO SHORT

Scenes designed to explain plot should be short. Information dumps that involve technical explanations should be short. Scenic descriptions that paint the background should be short.

WHEN TO GO LONG

Go long on scenes that include dialog. Readers like the white space. Plus, conversation reveals character. Go long on emotional scenes. If you lead with the heart and slowly reveal the longing, hurt, and fear, readers will turn the pages. Scenes of suspense should be revealed slowly. "Suspend." Hang your Lead on the edge and then leave him there.

If nothing is altered, you do not have a scene. If your characters solve something without a setback, you do not have a story.
~ STEVEN JAMES

SCENE PLACEMENT

Mix contrasting elements. If you have a long conversation scene, put a short descriptive scene after it. Follow an intense scene of heartfelt angst with a brief humorous scene. That gives the reader a chance to breathe. Think fight, regroup, fight, regroup. Another way to view the pacing of your scenes is with action, reaction, action, reaction.

SWEET SPOTS

Every scene has a "sweet spot," a moment that the rest of the scene points to. Find your scene's sweet spot and draw a box around it. Then read backward from there. Do the previous paragraphs build to the sweet spot? If not, cut or rework. When possible, place your sweet spot near the end of the scene.

POCKET SUSPENSE

Does this scene ratchet up the tension of the one before it? How can I make things worse?
~ STEVEN JAMES

Pocket suspense creates a pause in the action in order to reveal some other aspect of the story. For example, your Lead receives a college admission letter. Before she can open the envelope, her little brother causes the microwave to catch fire. This delay shows how irresponsible her brother is and why her parents want her to stay home and go to the community college. The answer of whether she'll get into the college of her choice is suspended while she deals with her brother, revealing both the character of both actors and building suspense.

OPENING YOUR SCENE

Where to begin: hook the reader. "Think of a scene as a blind date. The reader is the date sitting at the table waiting for you. You know the first words out of your mouth will set the tone for the rest of the evening. What do you say?" – **Raymond Obstfeld**

Bring on the bear: Open with a promise of danger.

Say what?: Begin in the middle of a conversation full of conflict, humor, or intrigue.

Big claim: Open with a big claim that hints at life changing events.

Action: Open in the middle of action, with movement leading to something dramatic. Car crash, kidnapping, etc...

Setting: If you begin your scene with a description of setting, then make sure the setting IS a character and not just backdrop.

Time: Open your scene with a focus on the time of day but add an element of surprise. "I woke up...with a horse head in my bed." "I'd just finished dinner... when Santa Claus fell down the chimney. "My head had just hit the pillow... when my wife told me she was leaving me.

Buddy System: Open a scene with someone else describing your Lead or another person.

Self-Description: In first person revelation show a characteristic of your Lead of which she isn't aware, like a tendency to exaggerate, for example, or self-loathing.

ACTION SCENES

An action scene is any scene where a character is trying to get somewhere, solve a problem, or move forward in the story. An action scene is when you have an objective, obstacles, and an outcome. The worse the scene ends, the better. Leave your lead in a worse position than he began.

REACTION SCENES

Reaction scenes are primarily about emotion. The scene flows from: Emotion (shock, fear, anger) Analysis (hide, call for help, run, wait) Decision (pick a path and move)

SETUP SCENES

A setup scene prepares the story for the next scene. It must have all the elements of a scene, including conflict. Keep these scenes short and place them early in the story.

QUESTION TO ASK FROM YOUR SCENES

- What can make the situation worse for my Lead?
- What part of my concept is familiar?
- Can I set this scene in a different setting?
- What trait could my Lead possess that hurts him?
- How can I make the characters in conflict hate each other?
- How can I make the characters in love be on opposite sides?

IN CONCLUSION

Every scene should have one or more of the following:
- Inner conflict
- Emotional indecision
- Outer conflict
- Obstacles to Lead's objective
- Tension fueled by:
  - Uncertainty (character doesn't have enough information)
  - Worry (character has unsettling information)
  - Doubt (character doesn't have confidence in her abilities or the circumstances)

FINALLY

A story is just one scene after another. Picture the setting, the characters. Listen to them breathing and the cadence of their speech. Study the thing they're shielding behind their back. Force them to reveal it. Paint the scene in short strokes and vivid colors. Make sure the character's goal is clear. Then film your characters as they act.

If your protagonist can solve a problem right away, it's only an event that might lead to a story, not the story itself.
~ STEVEN JAMES

Novels by Eddie Jones

Dead Man's Hand
Skull Creek Stakeout
Dead Low Tide
The Curse of the Black Avenger
Bahama Breeze

Chapter 5

Writing Romantic Comedy

How to Write the Romantic Comedy

Romantic comedies are light-hearted, humorous stories that demonstrate how true love can overcome all obstacles. In a typical romantic comedy, the two lovers tend to be young, likable, and apparently meant for each other, yet they are kept apart by complicating circumstances.

A happy ending is always the result.

The Basic Romantic Comedy Plot

The basic romantic comedy storyline involves a man and a woman who meet, part ways due to differences, then ultimately reunite.

Once the hero and heroine become involved, they must confront challenges that threaten to drive them apart. Sometimes they are reluctant to become romantically involved because they believe they do not like each other, one of them already has a partner, or because of social pressures.

Readers know from the beginning that the pair will get together—even if the couple does not—and that is part of the appeal of a romantic comedy.

OPPOSITES ATTRACT

The couple often seeks time apart to sort out their feelings or deal with the external obstacles driving them apart.

While they are separated, one or both usually realizes that they are ideal for each other, even though they are complete opposites. Then, one or both make some heroic effort to find the other person and declare their love, often just missing each other. (He flies to meet her; she does likewise. Each arrives at the other's house only to find that no one is home.)

Finally, the couple unites and one or both declare their love for the other. The story ends on a happy note.

BEGIN WITH LARGER THAN LIFE LEADS

To win the heart of your audience, your lead characters must possess certain endearing qualities:
- Empathy
- Shared goals, values, morals ...

- Perseverance
- Dishonesty

Note: *If* there is a romantic rival, introduce your hero *before* his romantic adversary appears on the scene. Readers and audiences instinctively identify with the first character they meet, and they will expect your Hero to appear early in the story.

EMPATHY FOR YOUR CHARACTERS

Readers want to fall in love with your Hero and Heroine.

They want to root for him to win her heart. When you write a romantic comedy, you must persuade the reader that these two are destined to be together—even when the reader knows a train wreck is coming.

Readers want to identify with the Heroine. If she comes across as a total jerk—even a misunderstood jerk—they won't pull for her.

Same with him. Without empathy, readers will lose interest in the story.

READERS WANT CHARACTERS WITH SHARED GOALS AND MORALS

Readers want your Heroine to ultimately win the heart of your Hero. If they don't long for these two people to head into the sunset together, you haven't properly cast the characters of your story. Your Hero and Heroine don't have to be Superman and Superwoman, but they should complement each other (i.e., providing skills and experience the other lacks, acting as the other's champion). In other words ... compliment each other. (As in, really saying nice things about the other, occasionally.)

PERSEVERANCE – INSURMOUNTABLE OBSTACLES MUST SEPARATE THE PAIR

The Hero and Heroine should demonstrate a focused determination to overcome insurmountable obstacles, whether they do so together or apart. This will leave readers cheering for the couple while, at the same time, wondering how they will ever make it together.

Overcoming these insurmountable obstacles bond the characters beyond their basic attraction to each other. (We all know teamwork can carry a couple long after the good looks go.)

Without overwhelming hurdles for the Hero/Heroine to overcome, the reader will be less likely to cheer for the couple. A mismatched pair is often a powerful formula for love.

DECEPTION – THE FIRST SIN

Romantic comedies always involve deception. The Hero/Heroine pretends to be someone he/she is not. Dishonesty increases the conflict and forces the heroes to confront their own internal needs, weaknesses, and fears.

Often the divide separating the hero and heroine is the result of deception. Once they face the truth about themselves, they may be able to change, grow, and get together.

ACTION AND OVERREACTION

The characters in a romantic comedy never think their situation is humorous. When readers are laughing, your Hero and Heroine are in pain. The couple's problems provide comic relief for readers.

Your story derives its humor from the way the pair *overreacts* to their situations. They concoct unbelievable solutions that only make their situations worse.

(Hiding behind fig leaves? Really? How *big* were those fig leaves?)

CHARACTER MOTIVATION

Establish your Hero/Heroine's external desires. Allow them to actually state their goal in the dialogue.

- What does he/she want outside of the central relationship?

- When *her* emotional desire clashes with *his* external goals, how is this conflict resolved? (Will he pick her over his career?)

- Does your Hero's external goal oppose the Heroine's? (i.e., she wants to be a Hollywood actress, and he's angling to become a Wall Street hedge fund manager.) One of them will have to sacrifice their dream — but which one?

OTHER PRIMARY CHARACTERS

Your story needs two supporting characters.

The NEMESIS prevents the hero / heroine getting what she wants. This can be a romantic rival or boss—anything that stands in the way of his/her goal.

The REFLECTION is the best friend or sidekick who knows the Hero better than he knows himself.

In romantic comedies, the REFLECTION will support the hero's desires, and the NEMESIS will oppose the hero.

NEMESIS and REFLECTION force your hero to grow and change over the course of the story.

INCITING INCIDENT

This is NOT the first meeting of your Hero and Heroine. It **IS** the event that sends his/her life spinning out of control.

What disturbing event disrupts the life/lives of your lead characters?

Your lead's inciting incident will alter their normal life and force them to face a new future.

CALL TO ACTION, DENIAL, REPEAT

- Challenge your Hero/Heroine to accept this new adventure or embrace this sudden turn of events.
- Show him/her refusing the challenge.
- Appeal to your Hero on an emotional level (i.e., "Look, Doc, I know after the malpractice suit, you swore you'd never pick up a scalpel again, but little Jimmy will die if you don't help.")
- Show your lead character's acceptance of the challenge.
- Begin the quest—your Hero/Heroine set off on their great adventure

ALL OF THE ABOVE HAPPENS BEFORE THE PAIR MEET!

1ST MEETING: A CHANCE ENCOUNTER

Both in real life and in fiction, that first meet is (or should be) a memorable moment.

Avoid cliché "bumping into each other." Aim the opposing external goals of your Hero and Heroine at the pair in such a way that they are forced to meet. (Competing bookstore owners—You've Got Mail, ad account rep, writer—How To Lose A Guy In 10 Days)

2ND MEETING: BACKGROUND REVEALED, VALUES PRESENTED, GROUND RULES ESTABLISHED

This is your Hero and Heroine's "getting to know you" encounter. Old wounds are revealed and shared hurts established. Each learns from the other where the boundaries are. (She's a vegetarian, his favorite dish is grilled venison. She gets seasick; he loves sailing.)

Like two boxers circling the ring, your Hero and Heroine size each other up and ... like what they see.

3RD MEETING: FIRST PHYSICAL ENCOUNTER

The first touch between the couple should set the hearts of readers beating with anticipation. (i.e., the touch of fingers as they reach for the same object; she loses her balance and falls against him.)

Aim for sensual versus erotic. He helps her into her coat and his finger brushes across her neck. Both pause, as if waiting for more, then an interruption ruins the moment.

Weave this scene into an external goal scene so that the focus isn't solely on the couple. In this way, when they touch, the reader is surprised by the result.

4ᵀᴴ Meeting: Falling for Each Other While in Pursuit of External Goals

Remember his/her outward motivation? Here we begin to see how their competing goals will drive your two lovebirds apart.

In this scene the two are physically together but mentally apart due to outside pressures. He's preoccupied with texting a response to his boss. She is multitasking while waiting for him to give her his drink order. Neither is focused on the other until some slight nudge forces them to pause and share a tender moment. Then it's back to work.

5ᵀᴴ Meeting: Surprises at Work

Having been so consumed by work earlier, one of the two decides to surprise the other at the office with flowers, lunch, etc. and interrupts an important meeting. This collision of two worlds creates new tension in the relationship.

Showing the Hero and Heroine in hostile territory often serves as a way to show how incompatible the pair is. The two can protect their persona outside of work, but on the job, the masks come down. This leads to conflict and ...

6ᵀᴴ MEETING: FIRST FIGHT

Now is the time for the couple's first hostile encounter. The reader saw this coming, even if the couple did not.

Differences are aired. What passed as acceptance turns out to courtesy and manners.

Let each of them state what they DO NOT like about the other, astonishing them both, leaving them reeling emotionally.

SECONDARY CHARACTERS

Enter the best friend, the mother, the understanding sister. This is the chance for your REFLECTION character to talk your Hero/Heroine off the ledge. Since he/she is speaking in confidence to a friend, this scene allows each to state what they DO like about the other, as well as what they detest without fear of inflicting further emotional pain.

Meanwhile, the heroine's NEMESIS will serve the role of Satan and plant doubts.

7ᵀᴴ MEETING: DOMESTIC ENCOUNTERS

The counsel of the secondary character has helped, and the Hero and Heroine manage to reconcile.

As a way of making up, they do something together in a domestic setting (i.e., cook a meal for a sick friend, babysit a niece or nephew). This "playing house" demonstrates to the reader and couple that they can serve as the foundation of a family. Turns out they are a great couple, after all.

POINT OF NO RETURN

The Hero and Heroine are now committed to the relationship. At this point, both make a physical, emotional and tangible commitment that indicates that he/her will pursue the other above all else.

From here on, neither of them can ever go back to their old life without returning with a broken heart.

8ᵀᴴ MEETING: GOALS DERAILED

External goals are not simply interrupted; now careers are threatened. Remember that job vacancy on Wall Street? They want to hire the Hero. Problem is, your Heroine just got a call back for a role in a new Netflix drama.

Meanwhile, a joint custody item (dog, youth soccer team, church outing) needs at least one of the two in attendance. Which one will make the sacrifice for the other?

Not her.

Not him.

FIRST TERMINATION

Now that they're committed, to one another and a new way of living/thinking, the real work of loving each other becomes too much.

Misunderstandings, work stress, cultural differences … all of it proves to be more than they can handle.

The reader saw this coming. Their friends saw it coming. Now the couple must face the truth: "We just weren't meant to be."

SECONDARY CHARACTERS STRATEGIZE TO KEEP THE COUPLE TOGETHER

REFLECTION friend(s) steps in to offer a new strategy for salvaging a relationship that is now obviously unraveling and becoming far too complicated.

This forces him/her to evaluate what's really important—career/goals, or her/him.

10TH MEETING: MEET THE FAMILY

Restore the relationship by bringing in the families. Allow a wise aunt, grandmother, etc. to explain how love is all about sacrifice for the other. Here is your chance to weave spiritual truth into your story (i.e., you cannot love purely without losing part of yourself).

He decides to skip the New York trip and do a Skype interview while dog-sitting her puppy. She'll be

back in time to take his place on the church Hab-
itat team so he can conference in with the Asian
office of the New York firm.

11ᵀᴴ MEETING: PROM NIGHT

Every good romance contains a Cinderella-at-The-Ball
 scene. All is going well, marriage may be an op-
 tion, small differences have been resolved. All that
 remains is The Commitment.
This is the moment the reader has been waiting for.
 Magic is in the air. We know they can make it now.
Then ...

SECRETS REVEALED

The clock strikes midnight. Real identities, secrets,
 motives are revealed. (secret sins, motives, faults)
Love is too hard. Can this ever work?

FINAL TERMINATION

"You go your way, I'll go mine."
"Fine."
"Fine!"

THE CHASE SCENE

The Hero or Heroine comes to their senses and realizes he/she can't live without the other. He/she

will never be complete without her/him. Nothing else matters.

Foregoing career, family, friends, future, the Hero or Heroine sprints to catch the other before it's too late.

IT'S TOO LATE

She/he is gone.
Emotionally checked out.
Circumstances have changed.

Time to move on.

12TH MEETING: THE FINAL ENCOUNTER

Not so fast.

Win or lose love. One or both must offer a sacrifice to demonstrate they are ready to abandon their former life in order to create a new life together.

13TH MEETING: TYING UP THE LOOSE ENDS

The happy couple sails into the sunset. Storms and problems lie ahead, but readers know this couple will face them down together.

Chapter 6

WRITING THE COZY
MYSTERY

HOW TO WRITE THE COZY MYSTERY

Despite changes within the book publishing indus-
try, cozy mysteries remain popular. Cozy mysteries allow readers to fall in love with a quirky
sleuth (Monk, Colombo, Patrick Jane) while at the
same time solving a puzzle. Cozies avoid profani-
ty, graphic violence, and overt sexual scenes. For
readers, the payoff has less to do with "who done
it" and more to do with "how the who done it."

WHAT IS A COZY MYSTERY?

A cozy mystery features an amateur sleuth solving a
murder within the confines of a controlled setting

(think train, mansion, small town). Most of the suspects know each other and thus know each other's secrets. This leads to lots of accusations as to whom the killer might be.

While murder is the key focus of the story, the characters, their relationships, and the setting, are what set the writer apart and thus, create reader loyalty.

THE COZY MYSTERY SLEUTH

The cozy mystery sleuth is usually an intuitive, bright individual forced to become an amateur sleuth due to circumstances. She/he is usually college educated with a real job—i.e. a dog trainer, homemaker, teacher … nun—with enough life experience to help her/him glean insights where other "professionals" may fail.

The amateur sleuth is usually a very likable person who is able to get the community members to talk freely (i.e. gossip) about each other. There is usually at least one very knowledgeable, nosy, and reliable character who is able to fill in all of the blanks, thus enabling the amateur sleuth to get a jump on the case. In fact, your sleuth will often be one step ahead of the authorities.

The amateur sleuth may face danger during the course of her/his investigation but rarely are they taken hostage or assaulted—only threatened.

Now let's kill someone.

SHOW THE BODY

Disclose the crime and mystery to be solved. The body must appear by the end of chapter one. On TV, the crime and body usually appear by the end of the first scene.

The crime must capture the reader's imagination. It should be committed in such an extraordinary way that either the victim or crime strike the reader as larger than life. "This is no ordinary murder." Give the reader enough information about the victim to make them truly care that the perpetrator be captured and justice served. (High-ranking official, politician, sports star, dot-com millionaire.)

INTRODUCE YOUR SLEUTH

Show your amateur sleuth doing or saying something very clever or unexpected as she/he stands over the body which will establish her/him as unique. Create this character with care. Your sleuth must be interesting enough to hold the reader's attention throughout the book.

It is not necessary to disclose all aspects of her/his personality in the opening scenes. Back-story will come out through subplot. **Do** reveal enough details to allow the reader to bond with your main character (single mom, widow, cancer-survivor).

SET THE SCENE

Ground the reader in time and place. It is often useful
to include some sort of symbol, an object or a person, in the opening scene that serves as a metaphor
for the story (feather, flower, etc.). The reappearance of this symbol at the conclusion of the story
will hint at your story's theme.

Provide enough details about the gravity of the crime
to create compassion from the reader and ground
them in the story.

REVEAL CLUES

Reveal clues within the first few pages that suggest
both physical and psychological aspects of the
crime. Those clues should point to suspects and
motive.

Some clues should point the sleuth in the right direction, others will not. Stealth clues may not be recognized as actual clues until later in the story.

Three to five clues are enough to begin solving the
case.

INTRODUCE SUBPLOT

The plot will drive the story forward, but **the subplot carries the theme. Your theme** is a universal concept to which the reader can relate. (In
inspirational cozies this will be your spiritual mes-

sage.) (The murder of Able: sacrifice out of love, not duty.)

Subplots tend to originate in a crisis in the sleuth's private life and may involve an issue of character, such as courage or honesty. (i.e., the widowed amateur sleuth refuses to date for fear of falling in love and experiencing loss again.)

SELL THE SUBPLOT TO YOUR READER

The ultimate resolution of the subplot will demonstrate change or growth on the part of your sleuth. Her inner conflict will be resolved in a collision of personal and professional goals. (i.e., both external and internal goals will squeeze your sleuth to the breaking point.) That climax may coincide with, or occur as prelude to the climax of the main plot.

The subplot may be a vehicle for a romantic interest or a confrontation with personal demons of the sleuth. The author can manipulate the pace of the novel by moving back and forth between the plot and subplot.

What question does your sleuth want answered: that is her/his subplot dilemma.

SEND YOUR SLEUTH FORWARD

Set your sleuth on the path toward solving the case by presenting plausible murder suspects. All suspects appear to have some connection to the victim.

Have your sleuth question each one. Three to five suspects are enough to keep the reader guessing as to who the killer is.

One will turn out to be the killer, but most will have a secret that keeps them under suspicion until late into the story.

REVEAL FACTS ABOUT SUSPECTS

After the initial questioning, show your sleuth uncovering facts about each suspect that deepens her/his suspicion of each one. This can occur as she reviews their answers or through the discovery of new clues.

In a one-hour TV deductive show, all suspects are shown within the first 10 minutes. This allows viewers the opportunity to solve the case along with the sleuth.

Let the reader see your sleuth question each suspect's alibi, motive, and opportunity. As your sleuth processes what she's learned so will your reader.

RAISE DOUBTS ABOUT EACH SUSPECT

Give each of your suspects a secret that may or may not connect them to the victim. This will raise suspicions about each suspect.

Some of the secrets may reveal noble motives, such as leaving a trail of canceled checks marked "cash" that are used to support an undocumented cousin from Mexico. Or they may involve criminal activity that has nothing to do with the murder. Many of the suspects might wish the victim dead, but only one or two have actual motive.

Assign alibis for some but not all suspects. In TV shows, the suspect *without* an alibi *is usually not* the killer. He's simply a red herring. Some may be hesitant to reveal their whereabouts, while others may lie about where they were at the time of death (to protect sins and secrets). Still others may offer an alibi that contradicts something they or someone else said.

COMPLICATE THE CASE

About one-third of the way through the story, something should occur which makes it clear to the sleuth and reader that the crime is more complicated than originally thought. This often involves a revealed secret about the victim.

Hints may be given to allow the reader to actually see possibilities not yet known to the sleuth.

REVEAL YOUR SLEUTH'S BACKGROUND

The sleuth's background is revealed as the subplot is developed. Tell the reader what drives your sleuth, what haunts her or what is missing in her life. These are your sleuth's Internal goals—the things she wants to change about herself, but cannot or will not. Readers want to solve the puzzle, but they also want to cheer for someone for whom

they have empathy. The more heroic and vulnerable your character, the more deeply will be the
reader's bond with her.

Through a threat to her life or the revelation of a personal matter, make it clear that the sleuth has a
stake in solving the case.

This is how a series is made.

KILL OFF YOUR MAIN SUSPECT

At the mid-point of your story you may wish to kill off
the main suspect.

If you have placed the appropriate amount of suspicion
on the primary suspect, your sleuth and the reader
will be thrown off balance by this sudden death. If
you want to ratchet up the tension, first reveal that
your main suspect fled. Then show the body.

This lets the sleuth know she guessed wrong—that the
killer remains at large.

And might kill, a third time.

RAISE THE STAKES

Develop a sense of urgency.

Announce that the time allowed to solve the case has
been greatly reduced.

Raise the stakes via a threat to the sleuth or someone
close to her.

Make it evident that if the case is not solved soon, there
will be terrible consequences for your sleuth. (She

may be run out of town, be fired from her job, shunned ...)

BROADEN THE INVESTIGATION

This is the pivotal point in the story where it becomes evident that the sleuth is on the wrong track. With the lead suspect dead, she is back to square one.

Broaden the investigation to include other individuals not included in the first round of interrogation. **This is a red herring, but the reader doesn't know this.**

Information gathered through new interviews or the discovery of physical evidence, should point toward the solution, although the solution may not yet be apparent to your sleuth and the authorities.

REVEAL HIDDEN MOTIVES

Secret relationships come to light, such as business arrangements, romantic involvements, scores to be settled or previously veiled kinships.

Character flaws (sins) that kept suspects under suspicion are exposed, clearing them of the murder but showing them in a bad light.

If you want to make a social statement, use a suspect's immoral acts to make your point. (The golf pro is having an affair with his student, the bookstore manager embezzled money from her owner, the

track star is growing pot in the woods and that's
why there was dirt on his shovel.)

REFLECT UPON EARLIER CLUES

With your sleuth stumped as to who committed the
crime, show her carefully reevaluating the signifi-
cance of earlier clues.

Develop theories. Attach meanings to matters hinted
at in earlier interviews but discounted as unim-
portant.

STUMP YOUR SLEUTH

The sleuth considers everything she's uncovered about
the murder(s).

Misinterpretation of clues or mistaken conclusions has
led her in the wrong direction. With time running
out, she must apply logic and find a new way of
making sense of what she knows.

YOUR SLEUTH IN SOLITUDE

Show your sleuth reviewing the case in solitude.
Here, she will seek to determine where she went
wrong.

To the best of her knowledge, have her list the chain of
events that provoked the crime.

Crucial evidence presented at the beginning but over-looked now takes on new meaning in light of all the facts in the case.

The sleuth (and perhaps the reader, if a keen observer) becomes aware of the error that remains undis-closed to others involved in the case. This is your sleuth's "ah ha!" moment. Though the case still appears impossible, she is convinced she knows who the killer is.

SLEUTH SEEKS PROOF

Based on her deductive reasoning, your sleuth seeks positive proof of her yet undisclosed conclusion. She weighs the evidence and information gleaned from the other characters and carefully recreates the crime.

When others ask, she still does not reveal who the killer is. For that, all the suspects will have to gather in one place. This ensures the killer cannot escape.

RESOLUTION OF SUBPLOT

Your sleuth, having been tested by circumstances and challenged to change, is strengthened for final action. Old demons are cast out. Personal growth is expressed through her words and actions. We know she is a changed person, a better person.

But we still do not know who the killer is.

The Climax

A dramatic confrontation between the sleuth and the killer ensues in which the sleuth prevails.

The more "impossible" the odds, the more rewarding the climax will be. This scene can take place in a large room with all the suspects present (similar to the game of Clue: Professor Plum used a candlestick to kill Mr. Green in the kitchen) or in a solitary place where the killer may turn on your sleuth and threaten her.

If it's a solitary place, she will have already prepared a way out, perhaps alerting the sheriff in advance.

Resolution

Once your sleuth has escaped death and revealed the killer's identity, motive, and means of murder, we see the killer cuffed and taken away.

Next your sleuth explains what clues tipped her off to the killer and how she solved the case.

Last scene shows your sleuth enjoying the stated goal she longs for at the beginning of the story: a sailboat, vacation, chance to attend a writers' conference in the mountains ...

43198572R00056

Made in the USA
Middletown, DE
03 May 2017